Encyclopædia Britannica

Fascinating Facts

Dinosaurs

PUBLICATIONS INTERNATIONAL, LTD.

Encyclopædia Britannica, Inc.
310 South Michigan Ave.
Chicago, IL 60604

Printed and bound in USA.

8 7 6 5 4 3 2

ISBN: 1-56173-315-6

SERIES PICTURE CREDITS:

Academy of Natural Sciences; Allsport U.S.A.;
Animals Animals; Art Resources; Donald Baird;
John Batchelor; Blackhill Institute; Ken Carpen-
ter; Bruce Coleman, Inc.; Culver Pictures; Kent
& Donna Dannen; FPG International; Brian
Franczak; Howard Frank Archives/Personality
Photos, Inc.; Tony Freeman/PhotoEdit; Douglas
Henderson/Museum of the Rockies/Petrified
Forest Museum Association; Carl Hirsch; Blair
C. Howard; International Stock Photography;
Eleanor M. Kish/Canadian Museum of Nature,
Ottawa, Canada; Charles Knight/Field Museum
of Natural History; Vladimir Krb/Tyrell Mu-
seum; T. F. Marsh; NASA; Gregory Paul; Paul
Perry/Uniphoto; Christian Rausch/The Image
Works; Peter Von Sholly; SIU/Custom Medical
Stock Photo; Daniel Varner; Bob Walters; Peter
Zallinger/Random House, Inc.

The Age of the Dinosaurs

The Mesozoic era is divided into three periods: the Triassic (245-205 million years ago), the Jurassic (205-130 million years ago), and the Cretaceous (140-65 million years ago). Dinosaurs appeared at the end of the Triassic period and disappeared at the end of the Cretaceous.

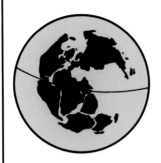  

Major Earth Changes

In the millions of years that dinosaurs were on the earth, the world underwent great changes. At first, all of the land was one big continent. Later, it broke up, causing mountains to form and seas to rise. Earth's climate changed, too. Swamps became deserts; flowers and trees appeared. As the earth changed, so did dinosaurs.

It's All in the Name

The word "dinosaur" comes from the Greek. *Dino* means "terrible" and *saur* means "lizard." It was probably coined as a name for these creatures because of their gigantic size.

Calling It by the Right Name

Dinosaurs are usually named after their distinguishing features or after the person who discovered their remains or where they were discovered. Interestingly enough, the scientist who named the *Apatosaurus* later named another dinosaur *Brontosaurus.* He later found out that *Brontosaurus* was just a larger *Apatosaurus.*

Dinosaur Discoverer

Gideon Algernon Mantell was a British paleontologist who discovered four of the five kinds (genera) of dinosaurs known during his time—*Iguanodon, Hylaeosaurus, Pelorosaurus,* and *Regnosaurus.*

Vertebrate Specialist ▼

Edward Drinker Cope discovered about a thousand species of extinct vertebrates (animals with backbones) in the United States. He is most noted for his knowledge on the vertebrates that flourished between the extinction of the dinosaurs (65,000,000 years ago) and the rise of man (2,500,000 years ago), part of which is known as the Tertiary Period of geologic time.

A Great Scholar ▲

Paleontologist Othniel Charles Marsh made extensive scientific explorations of the western United States and contributed greatly to knowledge of extinct North American vertebrates. In 1871, his group of scientists discovered the first pterodactyl (flying reptile) found in the U.S. He is credited with the discovery of more than a thousand fossil vertebrates and the description of at least 500 more. Marsh published major works on toothed birds, gigantic horned mammals, and North American dinosaurs.

Studying Fossils ▶

The study of fossils is important for at least three different reasons. First, the changes observed within an animal group are used to describe the evolution of that group. Fossils also provide geologists a quick way of assigning an age to the layer of rock in which they occur. Finally, fossil organisms may provide useful information about the climate and environment of the site where they were deposited and preserved.

Classifying Plants and Animals

Taxonomy is the science of classification of plants and animals. It compares what plants and animals are made of by methods of comparative anatomy and interprets differences and similarities through comparative genetics, biochemistry, physiology, embryology, behavior, ecology, and geography.

Apotosaurus fossils were used to reconstruct this skeleton

The Highest Grouping

Kingdom, divided into *Animalia, Plantae,* and others, is the highest grouping of taxonomy. After this comes the phylum, class, order, family, genus, and species.

Plants of the Dinosaur Age

In the latest part of the Triassic and in the Jurassic geological periods, the early dinosaurs lived in a world of conifers, ferns, and seed ferns. In the middle of the Cretaceous, new plants evolved. The familiar flowering plants and trees that we know appeared. Later dinosaurs fed on magnolia, laurel, dogwood, rose, oak, willow, birch, and others.

The Controversy Goes On

Years ago, scientists believed that all dinosaurs were cold-blooded. Recent studies have led some *paleontologists* (scientists who study fossils) to conclude that at least some dinosaurs were warm-blooded. Even though the controversy is still unresolved, scientists now agree that, contrary to the popular belief that dinosaurs were sluggish and slow-moving, many were fast and had high rates of metabolism.

All in the Family

Dinosaurs were reptiles and their closest living relative is the crocodile.

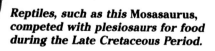

Reptiles, such as this Mosasaurus, competed with plesiosaurs for food during the Late Cretaceous Period.

Ruling the Seas

Two large groups of reptiles, the ichthyosaurs and the plesiosaurs, ruled the seas during the time of the dinosaurs. They were neither related to each other nor to dinosaurs.

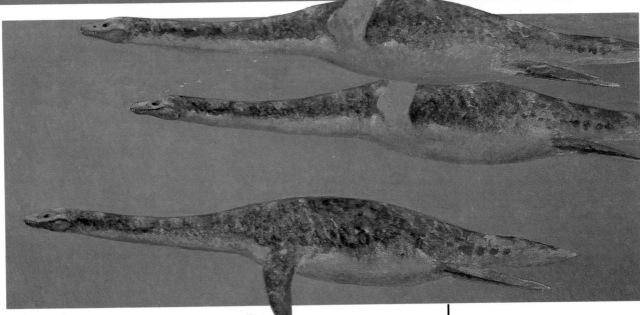

Marine plesiosaurs were meat-eating reptiles.

A Tough Survivor

Teleosts, or bony fish, were the most successful marine vertebrates of the Late Cretaceous Period. The shark, which was dominant during this time, has survived and changed little since the Mesozoic era.

Mothering Dinosaurs

Female dinosaurs probably laid eggs and sat on them or covered them with sand to keep them warm until they hatched.

Living Together

For many years, scientists believed that dinosaurs lived by themselves. New discoveries of bones and nests suggest that many dinosaurs lived in groups— like elephants and antelopes today.

Streamlined Bodies ▶

Ichthyosaurs from the Jurassic Period were very well known. Their bodies were streamlined and they had no distinct necks. Their heads blended smoothly into their bodies. These animals propelled themselves by means of well-developed, fishlike fins and by up and down movements of the body.

Fish Eaters

Ichthyosaurs were about 10 feet (3 m) long and were probably able to move through the water at high speeds. They probably fed on fish and other marine animals.

Animals of the Sea

It is unlikely that ichthyosaurs ventured upon the land. If stranded on shore, they must have been as helpless as modern beached whales and porpoises.

Made for the Water

Ichthyosaurs had very large eyes with their nostrils positioned far back on top of the skull. These made them very comfortable in the water and protected them from the water's pressure.

Long and Slender ▲

Nothosaurs were marine animals with long slender bodies, long necks and tails, and long limbs. They probably swam through the water whipping their long, slender necks in pursuit of fleeing fish. This early marine animal probably evolved from terrestrial reptiles.

Valuable to Scientists ▶

Ammonoids are very well-known marine invertebrates from the Mesozoic Era. Their straight or coiled, many-chambered forms are valuable to scientists who want to determine the age of things found from this time. They are relatives of the pearly nautilus and flourished in great diversity.

Pearly nautilus

A Long and Flexible Neck ▶

Plesiosaurus was about 15 feet (4.5 m) long, with a broad and flat body and relatively short tail. The neck was long and flexible. It had large teeth and nostrils far back near the eyes.

Feeding on Fish

Plesiosaurus probably ate by swinging its head from side to side through a school of fish. Apparently, it was able to use its large, paddlelike limbs to swim backward or forward or even to rotate itself.

Two Types of Reptiles

The early marine reptiles of the Jurassic and Triassic called plesiosaurs split into two main groups. Pliosaurs, the short-necked forms, had short necks and elongated heads. The elasmosaurs had relatively small heads and flexible snakelike necks.

Modern sturgeon

Longer and Longer

As plesiosaurs developed, they grew in size. *Kronosaurus*, an early pliosaur from Australia, was about 40 feet (12 m) long. The skull alone was 12 feet (3.7 m) long. *Elasmosaurus* had as many as 76 vertebrae in its neck and reached a length of about 43 feet (13 m). Fully half of it consisted of the head and neck.

A Primitive Fish ▲

The most primitive form of the bony fishes was the *Chondrosteiformes*. They are represented in modern times by sturgeon.

◄ Early Fish

The holost fishes replaced the chondrosts, but they declined in numbers and only a few forms, such as the Mississippi garpike, survived them.

Similar to Crocodiles

Phytosaurs were heavily armored semiaquatic reptiles that lived in the Late Triassic. They are not ancestors to modern crocodiles, although they probably resembled them and had similar habits. Their long and pointed jaws had numerous sharp teeth; phytosaurs probably preyed upon fish.

Finding Fossils

Phytosaur fossils occur in North America, Europe, and India, but their remains have not been found in the southern continents.

Opening Its Mouth Underwater

The nostrils of a phytosaur were high on its skull near its eyes. This allowed it to open its mouth underwater without drowning.

A Long Skull

Rutiodons were a type of phytosaur that was more than 10 feet (3 m) long; its skull alone was 3.5 feet (1 m) long.

A Very Good Mother

One duckbilled dinosaur named *Maiasaura*, whose name means "good mother dinosaur," cared for her young even after they hatched. Fossil remains of baby *Maiasaura* teeth suggest that they had been eating tough plants, which the mother must have brought to their nest. By taking care of her babies, this dinosaur ensured their survival.

Breaking an Egg

Dinosaur eggs were not large. The largest ones were only 10-12 inches (25-30 cm) long and had thin shells. Eggs were small so that baby dinosaurs would be able to break their way out.

Evolving Reptiles

Archosaurs, or "ruling reptiles," were spectacular early reptiles. At first, they had crocodilelike forms and lived in the water. When they invaded the land, their strong hind legs and swimming tails allowed them to stand up on two feet. Dinosaurs developed from these reptiles.

From Reptiles to Birds ▲

Pterosaurs could not really fly because of their large, spreading wings. They glided instead, launching themselves from high places. Competition from birds may have hastened the extinction of the pterosaurs.

Mini Mammals

Mammals that lived during the age of dinosaurs were small, mouselike, and insignificant. After the disappearance of dinosaurs, they evolved and eventually took over the earth.

Reptiles that Fly

Some archosaurs developed into pterosaurs, which were flying reptiles that resembled birds but had broad leathery wings. Instead of feathers, they were covered with hair. Their wings were supported on an enormous fourth finger. *Quetzalcoatlus* had a wingspan of 39 feet (12 m).

The First Bird

The first known bird from the Jurassic Period (150 million years ago) was the *Archaeopteryx*. It resembled a small dinosaur with feathers. The many bird types that we have today developed from this creature.

Dinosaur Types

There were two main types of dinosaurs that were categorized by the way that their hips were arranged. One group was called lizard-hipped; the other—bird-hipped. Lizard-hipped dinosaurs were either meat-eaters or plant-eaters. The meat-eaters were fierce and walked around on two legs. Some were very small. *Compsognathus*, for example, was no bigger than a chicken. Others were very large. *Deinonychus* was about the size of a man, but the resemblance ended there. It had a huge, sicklelike claw on its hind foot, which it used to attack other animals. *Tyrannosaurus* was the largest meat-eating dinosaur. It was 40 feet (12 m) long!

Tyrannosaurus rex

Mostly Like Bats ▶

Pterosaurs are members of a group of flying reptiles that flourished in the Jurassic and Cretaceous Periods of the Mesozoic Era. Like bats rather than birds, pterosaurs formed a wing surface by means of a membrane of skin. Unlike in bats, however, the membrane was attached solely to the fourth elongated finger. From there it extended back along the flank to the knee; a second membrane lay between the neck and the "arm." The first three fingers were slender, clawed, and good for clutching.

Large Brains ▼

The brains of pterosaurs were large and apparently comparable to those of birds. Sight rather than smell seems to have been the dominant sense.

One Type of Pterosaur

Rhamphorhynchus had strong, sharply pointed teeth, relatively short bones supporting the fingers, and a long tail with a diamond-shaped rudder at its tip. Its wingspan was about 2 feet (0.6 m).

A Very Small Pterosaur

Pterodactylus was a small reptile, in some cases no larger than a sparrow. Features included a few small teeth, long finger bones, and a short tail.

The Largest Flying Animal

Descendants of the *Pterodactylus* continued on into the Cretaceous Period and were much larger. Parts of three very large specimens were discovered in Big Bend National Park, Texas, in 1975. The wingspan of the largest specimen was about 51 feet (15.5 m), making it by far the largest flying animal of which there is knowledge.

From Reptiles to Mammals ▲

Therapsids were reptiles of the Permian and Triassic Periods that developed into mammals. Among meat-eating therapsids, gorgonopsians and therocephalians were characteristic of the Permian, and cynodonts and bauriamorphs were later representatives.

A Small Dinosaur ▲

During the Late Jurassic there was a small dinosaur in Europe called a *Compsognathus*. It was only as large as a modern chicken. It was lightly built and able to move very fast on its two strong hind limbs. Its forelimbs were suitable for grasping.

Very Salty Water

Some scientists believe that the oceans during the Late Permian were extremely salty. Very little marine fauna were present at the time.

A Very Fierce Creature

Tyrannosaurus, whose name means "tyrant lizard," had tiny front limbs and a huge skull with many sharp teeth that were very good for biting and tearing. Its teeth were six inches long and an inch wide. Their edges were ragged like a steak knife. This creature was powerful enough to attack any of its contemporary dinosaurs!

Walking Along

Unlike meat-eating dinosaurs that walked on two legs, plant-eating dinosaurs generally walked on four legs.

Some Very Big Dinosaurs

Plateosaurus was one of the first plant-eating lizard-hipped dinosaurs. It had a very long neck and could walk on either two or four feet. This creature could eat both meat and plants. Some of the dinosaurs that this creature developed into were truly amazing. *Diplodocus*, for example, was 87 feet (27 m) long with a long neck and long tail. The *Brachiosaurus* and its relatives were even bigger. Some actually were 100 feet (30 m) long and weighed 165 tons. *Brachiosaurus* is the largest known dinosaur.

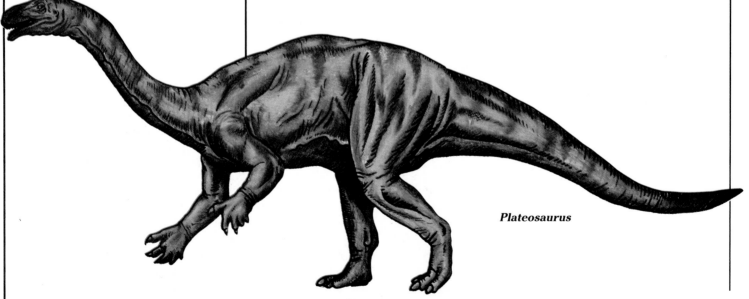

Plateosaurus

The Longest Land Animal ▲

Diplodocus of the Late Jurassic in North America was the longest land animal that ever lived. The longest one found was 87.5 feet (26.7 m). Its skull was unusually small, elongated, very light, and sat atop a very long neck. Its brain was extremely small. The tail was very long and probably extremely flexible. It is possible that its tail was a defensive weapon that could be lashed out at predators with great force; it is also possible that it was used to move through water.

Eating Soft Vegetation

The pencillike and dull-edged teeth of *Diplodocus,* as well as their location, indicate that this animal probably fed on soft vegetation.

Not a Second Brain

Because *Diplodocus* had such a long body, transmission of nervous impulses from its tiny brain to the hindquarters was a very slow process. As a result, a spinal node—often mistakenly called a second brain—was developed to compensate for the time lag.

Spending Time ▶ in Water

Diplodocus probably spent a great deal of time in the water with its head sticking out. It may have moved around freely on dry land; its limbs were stout and the feet broad, much like those of the modern elephant.

A Very Large Animal

Apatosaurus, found in the Late Jurassic Period, was one of the largest land animals of all time. It weighed as much as 30 tons and was as much as 70 feet (21 m) long, including its long neck and tail. It had four massive and pillarlike legs.

Change of Opinion

The size, shape, and features of the *Apatosaurus* head were disputed for more than a century. At first, the head was thought to be a massive, snub-nosed skull with spoonlike teeth. In 1978, scientists concluded that the animal had a slender, elongated skull with long, sharp teeth.

Maximum Size

It is probable that *Apatosaurus* represents the maximum size and bulk that a land animal can attain before becoming aquatic (a sea animal).

All for Defense

It is likely that the long and powerful tail of *Apatosaurus* was its main defense and that it sought refuge from pursuers by retreating to the water.

Walking on Two Legs

Allosaurus walked on two legs and had very strong hind legs. Its forelimbs, or arms, were much smaller than its hind limbs and were probably used for grasping. They had three fingers ending in sharp claws. The skull of the *Allosaurus* was very large in relation to its compact body and was lightened by the presence of several large openings.

Eating Other Dinosaurs ▶

It is probable that *Allosaurus* preyed upon the medium-sized dinosaurs, especially the duck-billed forms. It may have also been a scavenger, feeding upon carcasses of dead or dying animals. *Allosaurus* may have hunted in groups.

An Enormous Tail ▲

Allosaurus was a meat-eating dinosaur that weighed 2 tons and grew to 34 feet (10.4 m) in length, half of which consisted of a well-developed tail that probably functioned as a counterbalance for the body.

Big Plant ▶ Eaters

Sauropods, or plant-eating dinosaurs, generally had massive bodies, strong limbs to support their massive weight, long tails and necks, and a small head. The larger sauropods spent most of their time feeding on vegetation.

Adept at Eating Plants

The *Iguanodon* was the first dinosaur to be discovered in the early 19th century. It was a bird-hipped dinosaur that had birdlike feet. As all bird-hipped dinosaurs, this creature only ate plants. It had no teeth at the front of its jaw—only a bony beak. Its cheek teeth, however, were bony and rigid. This creature probably pulled plants into its mouth with its tongue, and nipped them off with its beak.

It's All ◀ in the Head

Duckbilled dinosaurs belonged to the plant-eating group. They all had long heads that ended in front with broad, flat bills. Some had different sizes of crests made of bone; others were flat-headed. Duckbilled dinosaurs ate plants, twigs, and pine needles. As their teeth wore down, they grew new ones.

Frills and Horns

Triceratops, a large plant-eating dinosaur of the Late Cretaceous, had a massive body (25 feet (8 m)) long, very long skull, large bony frills around the neck, and three long, pointed horns—one on the nose and two longer ones above the eyes.

A Sizable Skull

The horns above the eyes of *Triceratops* were more than 3 feet (1 m) long, and the skull alone was sometimes more than 6 feet (2 m) long.

A Heavy Dinosaur

It has been estimated that *Triceratops* must have weighed as much as eight or nine tons when fully grown. These creatures traveled in groups or small herds.

Fit for Eating Plants

The mouth of *Triceratops* was beaklike in the front and probably effective for nipping off vegetation. The cheek teeth could effectively chew plant material. The skeleton was massive, the limbs were very stout, and the feet ended in stubby toes probably covered by small hooves.

Now That's a Lot of Teeth ▶

Duckbilled dinosaurs, or hadrosaurs, had ducklike snouts and very large numbers of teeth. Some of these creatures had as many as 2,000 teeth that they used for grinding hard vegetables.

Making Noise ▲

Corythosaurus was a duckbilled dinosaur that appeared at the end of the Cretaceous Period. Its nasal tubes ran from the nostril on the snout up into the crest and then down again into the mouth. This dinosaur may have used this complicated breathing system to make loud sounds and honks.

One of the Last to Go ▼

Triceratops was the largest horned dinosaur. It looked a bit like a rhinoceros with its heavy head shields and defensive horns mounted on its face. This creature was one of the last dinosaurs to disappear.

Armored Dinosaurs ▲

Other types of bird-hipped dinosaurs had armor. Stegosaurs—*Stegosaurus* is the best known—had rows of plates and spikes down their backs. Ankylosaurs were squat creatures with plates covering their backs, their heads, and their tails. *Scolosaurus* was a famous ankylosaur. They were all peaceful plant-eaters that moved slowly.

Large Animal with a Small Head ▶

Stegosaurus was an armored dinosaur of the Late Jurassic Period. It reached a length of about 20 feet (6.5 m). Its skull and brain were very small for such a large animal. *Stegosaurus* had forelimbs that were much shorter than its hind limbs, giving its back a very arched appearance. Its feet were short and broad.

Controlling Body Temperature

Stegosaurus had a series of large, triangular, horn-covered bony plates along its tail and back. Originally, scientists thought that these plates served a defensive purpose. In the 1980s, they began to think that these plates may have helped *Stegosaurus* control or modify its body temperature. By positioning itself so that the plates faced the sun, *Stegosaurus* could have warmed itself. Similarly, by standing so that the plates were not struck by direct sunlight, the dinosaur could have avoided overheating.

Spiky Tail

There were pairs of long, pointed spikes on the tail of *Stegosaurus*. These were probably used as a lethal weapon. *Stegosaurus* was a plant eater, probably feeding on soft vegetation.

◄ Catching its Prey

Ornitholestes was about 6 feet (2 m) long and had a very flexible neck. Its forelimbs were very well developed and ended in fingers longer and slimmer than are common in dinosaurs. This indicates that *Ornitholestes* could catch quick-moving and elusive prey.

The Bird Robber

It has been suggested that *Ornitholestes* may have preyed upon the early birds, hence the name, which means "bird robber." It is equally probable that it ate small, speedy lizards and even early mammals.

A Complete ► Skeleton Found

A small, lightly built dinosaur found as fossils in Late Jurassic deposits of North America was *Ornitholestes*. It is relatively well known, since a complete skeleton was found in Wyoming.

Walking on Two Legs

Pachycephalosaurus was a dinosaur of the Cretaceous Period. It grew to be about 30 feet (9 m) long, walked on two legs, and had strong hind limbs and much less developed forelimbs.

A Domelike Skull

The unusual and distinctive feature of *Pachycephalosaurus* was the high, domelike skull formed by a thick mass of solid bone growth over the tiny brain. Abundant bony knobs in front and at the sides of the skull further added to its unusual appearance.

Bone-headed Dinosaurs

Pachycephalosaurus and closely related forms are known as the bone-headed dinosaurs.

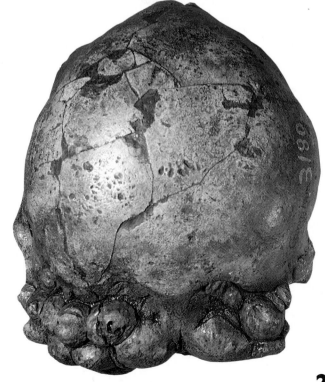

Bony Plates and a Club

The back of the low, flat body of the *Ankylosaurus* was covered with bony plates that were pointed at the flanks of the animal. At the end was a thick knob of bone that could have been used as a club.

Different Kinds of Armor

Some relatives of *Ankylosaurus* had different kinds of armor. Some varieties had long, pointed bony spikes at the end of their tails. Others had spikes of bone in the shoulder region.

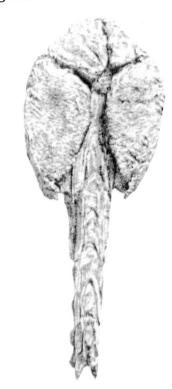

Wearing Armor

Ankylosaurus was an armored dinosaur of the Late Cretaceous Period of North America. It was about 15 feet (5 m) long, with hind limbs larger than the forelimbs.

An Amazing Neck

The small, light skull of *Struthiomimus* was perched atop a long, slender, and very flexible neck. The forelimbs were long and slender. The three-fingered hand had sharp claws adapted for grasping.

Egg-eater

The jaws of *Struthiomimus* were toothless and probably covered with a rather birdlike horny beak. Some scientists believe that this dinosaur fed upon the eggs of other dinosaurs.

Like an Ostrich

Struthiomimus was an ostrichlike dinosaur of the Cretaceous Period in North America. It was about 8 feet (2.5 m) tall, walked on two legs, and was adept at rapid movements on well-developed and strong hind limbs with three-toed, very birdlike feet.

Primitive Members

Protoceratops were dinosaurs of the Late Cretaceous Period. They were found in the Gobi Desert in Mongolia. They were one of the most primitive members of the last major group of dinosaurs to evolve.

Bony Frills on the Skull

Protoceratops was a relatively large animal. Adults were about 7 feet (2 m) long and weighed about 400 pounds (180 kg). The skull was very long. Bones in the skull had grown backward into a perforated frill that probably served as a surface for the attachment of chewing muscles and for shielding the vulnerable neck region from attack by predators.

Part Aquatic

The jaws of *Protoceratops* were beaklike and contained some teeth. A wrinkled area on top of the snout of the fossil may mark the position of a hornlike structure. The tail was well developed, suggesting that *Protoceratops* was at least part aquatic.

All Kinds of Remains

The remains of more than 80 individual *Protoceratops* have been found in all stages of growth. The eggs, about 6 inches (15 cm) long and oval in shape, appear to have been laid in circular clusters.

28

◄ A Well-known Bird

Hesperornis is an extinct genus of birds found as fossils in Cretaceous deposits. It is the best-known bird of the Cretaceous Period. It combines primitive and advanced characteristics.

A Very Active Bird ▲

The legs of *Hesperornis* were powerfully developed and clearly adapted for rapid diving and swimming through the water. The neck was long and slender and the head smallish; both were probably capable of side-to-side movements. *Hesperornis* was clearly an actively swimming bird that probably chased and caught fish.

Early Beak

Teeth were present in the back of the lower jaw of *Hesperornis*. It has been suggested that the horny beak that has come to be characteristic of birds was in the process of formation in the front part of the jaw.

29

A Dinosaur Site

Dinosaur National Park in northwestern Colorado and northeastern Utah was set aside in 1915 to preserve rich fossil beds that include dinosaur remains. It covers an area of 211,061 acres (85,416 hectares).

Disappearing Animals

Dinosaurs are not the only type of animal that is extinct. Scientists estimate that 90 percent of all the animal species that have ever lived on earth are extinct.

Shrinking in Size

For a long time, the only land animals were reptiles. Among these were the dinosaurs. Strangely, most dinosaurs were very large in size, although their brains were quite small. After dinosaurs died out, reptiles developed into much smaller creatures.

Finding Dinosaur Remains

Dinosaur skeletons are often found as an assortment of bones left on top of the ground, when the rock they were fossilized in wore away.

Gathering Information

Reconstructing a dinosaur skeleton not only tells a scientist what the animal looked like. It also indicates how an animal moved and, from the chemical composition, what it ate.

Recreating a Dinosaur

When dinosaur fossils are found, uncovered bones are painted with varnish to harden them. Then, they are covered in a layer of plaster of Paris for protection. The entire rock the remains were found in is shipped to a museum in one piece, where the bones (or skeletons) are carefully chipped away from the rock. Again, the fossils are hardened with varnish and cemented together. Models are made for the missing pieces. Finally, after careful study, all of the pieces are fitted together to make a full-scale skeleton. Dinosaur skeletons can be seen in many major museums.

The Disappearance of Dinosaurs

At the end of the Cretaceous Period (about 65 million years ago), all of the dinosaurs seem to have died out. With them, many other animals—including the swimming and flying reptiles of the time—also disappeared. This left the world to be populated by mammals.

◄ Changing the Climate

Some scientists believe that dinosaurs became extinct as a result of an asteroid or meteor with a 6-mile (10-km) diameter hitting the earth. If this happened, disturbance in the earth's climate may have occurred, killing off all living things.

A Continuing Debate ►

Many scientists believe that the extinction of dinosaurs was gradual and was, perhaps, due to changes in climate and geography. No one knows for sure and the debate continues.